Somebody Shoulda Told Me

Marriage, Do We Really Know What It's About?

Shelia,
Thank you for the support + love. I pray that you are blessed + highly favored.
Love
Remon & Candace Tuck

COPYRIGHT ©2015

SOMEBODY SHOULDA TOLD ME

REMON AND CANDACE TUCK

Editor: Julie B Cosgrove
Crossword Press

All rights reserved. No part of this book may be reproduced, stored in a retrieval system or transmitted, in any form or by any means, electronic, mechanical, photocopying, recording, or otherwise, without written permission of the authors, Remon and/Candace Tuck.

Cover art by: Ravsingh

Self-Published by: Remon & Candace Tuck

Unless otherwise indicated, all Scripture quotations in this publication are taken from the Holy Bible New International Version®(NIV) Copyright 1973,1978,1984
Printed in the United States of America

ISBN: 978-1-329-83334-0 (paperback)

Table of Contents

Acknowledgements

Introduction

What Is Marriage?

Chapter 1: Trust

Chapter 2: Communication

Chapter 3: Sex

Chapter 4: Infidelity

Chapter 5: Forgiveness

Chapter 6: Compromise

Chapter 7: Finance

Chapter 8: Expectations

Chapter 9: Quality Time

Chapter 10: God's Plan

ACKNOWLEDGEMENTS

We would like to take this time to thank all the people that made this book possible and played a crucial part in our marriage. Thank you to those that spoke life into our relationship by your words of encouragement, advice, compliments on our union, and perspective on our relationship. We would like to thank our families (parents, siblings, and cousins) for keeping it REAL. They told us when we were wrong, they told us when we were right, and asked questions that required us ponder how our actions may affect our marriage, spouse, and/or children. Thank you Mitchell and Elaine Tuck, for your wealth of knowledge and experience has been priceless. Thank you to my line sisters that gave me their opinions when I asked and when I didn't (only the Goddesses).

(Candace) Special thanks to my friend, Courtney Jackson, for planting a seed for me to write a book. Courtney after a conversation we had you said to me, "You need to write a book and I will buy it." Well here it is. I would like to thank Dawn Paul for watering the seed years later when I was posting topics and accumulating wins from my speeches given at my Toastmasters club. D.P. said to me, "Maybe one day these speeches will turn into a book." I never mentioned publicly that Courtney told me this and since I don't believe in coincidences, I know God was speaking to me.

Lastly, I must thank my husband for asking my hand in marriage. You have helped me be a better person. From college sweethearts to now. We might not have liked it each other on occasions, but we have turned our low experiences into life lessons that have placed our marriage on a mountaintop. Thank you for always supporting my goals and dreams, even participating in events you didn't necessarily want to do but did for me. I presented this book thing before and when it didn't work out you stepped up to the plate and said, "WE CAN DO IT!" After reflecting on this decision—this is the perfect way to do it--with my best friend, my lover, my soul mate. I've always said we are the same version of one another (with an exception or two) in the opposite gender body. We are not perfect--and our marriage is not perfect--but you are the perfect person for me!

(Remon)To my wife/Queen/best friend I would like to say thank you. Your love, forgiveness and passion have kept this marriage together. I pray God will continue bless you with all your heart desires. You have pushed me when I didn't want to be pushed. You have loved me when I didn't deserve your love. The man I inspire to be is all because I want to love my Queen in the fashion she deserves. I want the world to know my rib/ wife is the reason I strive to be a Kingdom Man, because a Queen deserves nothing else.

We are truly thankful to CrossWord Press for believing in our vision and dream. You have supported us from the beginning. You were heaven sent and a true blessing to us both.

INTRODUCTION

August 1995. Jarvis Christian College. Washington Hall.

The first day the city girl laid eyes on the country boy! Dressed in his ENTIRE high school basketball uniform, socks up to his knees (you know, Michael Cooper style). I was with my friends when he came into his friends dorm room to inform him he was about to do a run to Big Sandy. At first site he looked a hot mess to me. Fast forward to today, we have been together for twenty years, married for thirteen years and have three beautiful children together. In our thirteen years of marriage we have been madly in love, and then fallen out of love, but now we are growing and going stronger than ever before. We might not always like each other but our love for one another makes our relationship unyielding.

As with any married couple, we have experienced mountain highs and valley lows. Being lovers of music we would explain it this way. Most of our years sung *Nobody* by Keith Sweat. Oh, but don't you know some years sung *Let It Burn* by Usher. So how did we come from *Let It Burn* back to *Nobody*? By remembering the lyrics of Mary Mary hit song, *Can't Give up Now*. For those that are married, you know a marriage is like a rollercoaster. One minute you're up, the next minute you're down. You pull out from the gate...excited. As you go up the hill you are thrilled and screaming ecstatically anticipating the amazing ride. And just like a rollercoaster once you hit that first drop (in your marriage). It's gut wrenching, takes your stomach away, is terrifying, and shocking. Throughout the rest of your marriage you will have ups and downs and be looped all around.

Several years ago we hosted events in our home where married couples were able to socialize and dialogue about marriage. If you are married or have ever been married, you know this cohort is different from any other relationship you can have. It's one of those things you have to experience to be able to give input on it. These events allowed married folks to hang with other married folks with the purpose of escaping for a date night and be in a fun atmosphere, all the while engaging in meaningful conversations that allowed them to make "deposits" and "withdrawals" in their relationship so that it may be stronger and everlasting.

ಶಂಶ

Somebody Shoulda Told Me is a spin-off of these social gatherings. We decided to open up our hearts and share our journey with you. We hope it becomes apparent that all marriages have blemishes, but if you both commit to loving each other the best you can you can survive. The purpose of writing this book is to help married folks understand what it takes to grow together and avoid divorce court if possible. You are about to read about our personal experience and hear our personal opinions, but realize nothing stated is an absolute for every man, woman, or situation.

Each chapter begins with us sharing our mindset in the first several years of our marriage. This is followed by a question and answer conversation we had with one another. Our responses are identified by RT (Remon) and CT (Candace). The last part of the chapter is called **Somebody Shoulda Told Me** (SSTM) which states what we have learned over the past thirteen years through experience as well as God working in our marriage and through us individually. SSTM also offers advice to all married and engaged couples, and anyone thinking about getting married. Please allow our trials and tribulations to prevent you from possibly walking through the same fire.

FYI—this book is written in casual register. We decided to write in a conversational style because we felt like it would be more welcoming and entertaining. This style allows us to express our individual personalities and how we operate collectively. Therefore, it may not be, better yet it will not be, grammatically correct at times.

MARRIAGE—
DO WE REALLY KNOW WHAT IT'S ABOUT?

"That is why a man leaves his father and mother and is united to his wife, and they become one flesh."
Genesis 2:24

Candace (CT): Women begin dreaming about marriage at a young age. I'm sure it's soon after reading the story of Cinderella. Are boys even made to read the story of Cinderella?! But anyway. We start pointing out little boys we think we are going to marry. I'm sure it was a little girl that came up with the K-I-S-S-I-N-G childhood song, being fast. By our sophomore year in high school, we know the type of man we want to marry, how many kids we want to have, AND the type of house we want to live in. Meanwhile, we remain totally oblivious as to how marriage will grab us by our shoulders and shake the crap out of us. And while the women are fantasizing as little girls about getting married, the men's mindset are so far from the thought of marriage.

Remon (RT): We don't grow up thinking about marriage. Yes, one day we would like to have a wife and kids BUT again we are not thinking about getting married when we are a young boy, teenager, or young man. We don't grow up opposed to it either. It's that simple for us.

Remon & Candace Tuck   Somebody Shoulda Told Me

When you do get married you are seeing what you want to see. Either you picture it exactly like you saw it growing up or the exact opposite. Depending on the examples you saw growing up, you make a conscious decision to bring it in or leave it out of your marriage. AND THAT STILL DOESN'T PREPARE YOU! You don't really know what marriage is about. You have no earthly clue. Marriage can be both heaven and hell on earth. It has an on-the-job training requirement. Pre-marital counseling is a must. Counseling will give you a glimpse of what is circling around in the head of your future spouse.

But when you actually have to deal with certain issues after the wedding, your religion is tested and you wonder if you married who you really thought you did. One of the hard things about marriage is the smallest situations can become so huge. When you decided to marry your spouse you probably had the same morals, ethics, and religion but it's those minute things that can throw a monkey wrench in the game of love. When men get married we are thinking about what our wife is supposed to do. I can see my wife cooking. I envision her cleaning and keeping my house clean. And I know she will give me sex all the time. As a younger dude, you don't realize the importance of your role as a husband. The simplest decisions or wrong mindset can completely make a happy home a miserable abode in which to lay your head. These decisions can set it off for months, sometimes years. You don't realize this as a young dude. You are thinking it's going to be my way or the highway, kind of.

According to the CDC/NCHS National Vital Statistics System, the provisional number of marriages in 2014 in the United States was 2,140,272. On the downside of that there were 813,862 divorces/annulments in the same year. That means approximately half of our marriages are ending in a divorce. As we know there is not one specific reason that all these marriages fail, it is different for every couple. In our marriage we have experienced several of the common reasons people have ended their marriage and filed for divorce.

We will discuss some of the top issues that lead to divorce, and then see if we can find a solution in order to help more married couples' relationship last forever.

Chapter 1

TRUST

"There is no fear in love. But perfect love drives out fear, because fear has to do with punishment. The one who fears is not made perfect in love." John 4:18

Before you get married, one of the first things that establishes your relationship is trust. You trust that person enough to give them your heart, mind, and soul. Once you truly trust someone, you are willing to give all of who you are to them.

When people give of themselves they will move mountains for you, move across the world to lay in your arms every night, and sacrifice their goals and dreams to see you conquer yours. So when the trust in a marriage is broken, it shatters the core being of the person that trusted you with their heart. Trust is a necessity of your relationship. Trust is the nucleus of your relationship. If it is fragile or missing you must realize your marriage will eventually crumble. A lack of trust is a gateway to so many other problems such as a lack of communication, division, false accusations, and cheating. A lack of trust brings an unbalanced presence into your marriage.

Remon & Candace Tuck   Somebody Shoulda Told Me

Our personal story….

Trust issues affected our marriage. My foundation of trust was weakened when he would not be honest with me. Being an optimist I always give people the benefit of doubt. I see good until you've shown me differently, therefore when he told me things, I believed him. He is my husband and, the leader of our home so why wouldn't I believe him? When I found out that he was not being truthful about certain things it felt like I was hit with a body punch. It was very painful. I eventually got to the point where I started masking my pain with anger. His word no longer meant anything to me and I took it at half value. Then one day after finding out he had not told me the truth I felt the need to ask him if I was doing something that made him feel like he couldn't be honest with me. (I know lying is a choice, but in my reflecting moment I thought maybe I was making him uncomfortable or something). Of course, my counseling hat was on so I had other thoughts as to why this was happening and I'm pretty sure I was dead on about it. If I was unconsciously doing something to make him feel like he had to lie, I was willing to self-correct. I just wanted us to be happy and I wanted to be able to trust my husband.

The things that he was lying about were so minute that I couldn't figure out the purpose for not being honest with me. As his wife, I should be able to trust anything he tells me. He eventually told me that the reason he lied was because he didn't want to hear my mouth. Because I'm not the type of woman that cut you with words, curse you out, or flip out, my counseling assumptions were correct. I think what my husband failed to realize is that if I found out he was not truthful my reaction was going to be magnified because now we have to deal with two issues. First, why he did or didn't do what he was supposed to do PLUS now I have a million questions as to why he chose to lie to me. The truth allowed me to deal with the issue in a shorter time frame. Lying took me on a journey from being hurt, then mad, to thinking in an independent and single mindset, closing off my feelings, and not seeing my husband in a positive light. To be truthful, I felt like it was me against him.

My husband decided that being truthful and dealing with the consequences was not as bad as lying and causing our marriage to deteriorate. If you asked your spouse for something and now it has come to fruition, it is important to acknowledge when they make the change you requested. If you can harp on what they are not doing, you should be willing to praise them when change comes about.

I (Remon) lost trust in my wife during a time I was not working. If our marriage got in a bad state financially, I didn't think I could trust her to be there for me. What I mean by "be there" is that I didn't feel like she would be supportive and would leave me to fend for myself when I couldn't. Out of everything we have been through this has affected me the most. It changed my outlook on us and my view of her.

HOW DO YOU REGAIN TRUST ONCE IT'S LOST?

RT: Time, consistency, and forgiveness. <u>Time</u> is needed to put in the work to regain trust. <u>Consistency</u> of saying and doing the right things that in time will show your husband or wife that you are sincere and have changed in whatever area you lost their trust in. Regaining their trust means you lost it so that person has to be willing to forgive you or have enough <u>forgiveness</u> in their heart to allow you to regain it.

If I'm not going to forgive you for this and we are not going to stay together you don't have time. And if you don't have time you won't be able to show me through consistency that you have changed.

CT: I agree with you, baby, on needing time, being consistent, and being willing to forgive. During this time period of making a full circle and starting to trust again, you have to make sure you don't repeat the behavior that caused him or her not to trust you. That will not work if they are still in the healing phase.

RT: Basically while you are on probation!! (Candace starts laughing) No, I'm serious. When you get a job, and in this case your job is regaining your spouse's trust, you are on a 30, 60, 90-day probation before you are deemed worthy of your spouse returning his or her heart to you. During this "probationary" period, you can get let go. You can be fired, basically put OUT---of your house.

CT: You have to show your partner that you are sincere. You can never poo-poo a situation if your spouse is hurt. You surely can't get mad because they are "in their feelings". You should not give them space unless they request it because it will allow for you two to drift a part. It is important to re-ensure your spouse that you are apologetic. Both parties cannot shut down at the same time. I actually think it helps the recovery phase to move quicker.

RT: What's that?

CT: That you keep showing her she matters. That you're sorry. That you don't want her love missing from your life.

RT: I think that is the same for men.

CT: Men don't want to talk. Y'all don't want us saying anything to y'all, though.

RT: Women will not go as long as men will go with the silence I must agree.

CT: You have to care for that wound. Doctor it, clean it, and cover it up. To recommit the same offense is like ripping off the bandage and digging your finger in the open wound.

RT: Once you realize, better yet, IF you realize "I can't get past the hurt I am feeling" be honest with your spouse and let them know. The problem most men have is that we are instant gratifiers. We want it now, we gotta have it now.

CT: Y'all want what now?

RT: Almost anything! And I say that because when it comes to forgiveness, men struggle when the time frame of your healing takes too long. Whether it's three months, three weeks, or three days. Men are thinking, "why are you still tripping?" Sometimes we don't realize the pain we have caused, and all the while we are thinking and feeling, "she needs to get over this!" Yes, even when we are in the wrong. Men, we really need to be more understanding and realize that it may take our wives much longer than we expect before they can move past the hurt we've caused.

Somebody Shoulda Told Me

Marriage is not the fairy tale you grew up watching in movies and hearing from childhood stories. We never had an inkling of a clue that we would experience anything that we have dealt with in our marriage. Somebody shoulda told me trust is different when you are married versus when you are dating. When trust is broken as a "girlfriend" or "boyfriend" it will affect you. However, once you vow to give your heart and your whole being to someone in the presence of God, family, and friends, having your trust broken cripples your spirit. Somebody shoulda told me that the person you marry could and possibly will do something that will cause you not to trust them and how this betrayal will impact your marriage negatively if you don't know how to handle it. And that mistrust can stem from so many different things, not only cheating. Little things such as sneaking in new purchases to big things like addiction and adultery.

I (Remon) actually was told! I didn't realize the magnitude of it. The significance of it. The depth of it. My old man had several conversations with me regarding trust. He told me, "If you lose the trust of your woman you cannot be upset that she hasn't forgiven you and that she is taking a long time to get over it. You can't get upset, son."

I called him one time to vent because I was tripping that CANDACE was still tripping and he told me to "SHUT UP!" and was flat out mad at me. He said I was the one tripping the worse. He said, "You have to realize you hurt this woman and you're mad because she hasn't forgave you. SHUT UP!"

And to tell you the truth it pissed me off that he was mad at me. So I was told before and during our marriage. Although I was told, actually going through it was different. I didn't realize how serious it was. When you hurt your wife and lose her trust, it is a matter you must take to heart.

When you can look at her face and see the pain in which you caused, it should be an eye-opening moment. You don't go into the marriage thinking you will lose her trust. I didn't realize the crippling effect it could have on her and my marriage.

When you are young your mindset is more like "I'm sorry", "I'm not going to do it again", and "Okay. Get over it". As I became older and wiser the pain on my wife's face from any hurt I caused her actually started hurting me. If you truly love your spouse and you two are in sync, their pain should hurt you just as bad.

When your trust has been broken you should:
- Allow yourself time to heal
- Speak what's in your heart but don't intentionally try to kill their spirit with daggering words
- Don't hold on to the pain or hurt longer than needed
- Be willing to forgive

Today, we both have changed from where we use to be. I (Remon) couldn't believe I started the 2015-2016 school year without a job. We were back in the same situation we were in the past. This time Candace has supported me from the beginning to the end. She encourages me and loves on me all the same. We are even working at the same school now! I must admit my mindset is different this time around. I think because we have crossed these burning sands before we are both handling the situation totally different. We have vowed to stick together and do what is best for each other and our family. We know God is testing our faith and strengthening our spiritual and physical relationship.

Chapter 2

COMMUNICATION

"To answer before listening— that is folly and shame." - Proverbs 18:13

According to a recent study by the American Academy of Matrimonial Lawyers (AAML), communication problems were the number one reason for divorce in the United States. The study stated that about 67.5 percent of all marriage failed because of a breakdown of communication.

Communication is a major part of any relationship (i.e. marriage, job, friendship, etc.). You have to be able to discuss basic fundamental topics with your spouse. If you do not talk to each other, you cannot get an understanding about any issues or concerns. Communication helps you grow together. It helps you overcome your problems. If you do not communicate there cannot be a resolution. Avoidance does not make the problem or your feelings go away.

You cannot expect your spouse to know when you haven't told them. God didn't give any of us the super power of mind reading. After trust, communication is the next most important aspect of a marriage. Without communication you are not working through your problems you are simply co-existing. If your marriage is going to be blossom and grow, communication is a necessity. Communication to marriage is like sunshine to a flower.

Communication allows a couple to be in unison. You should be able to discuss everything from family affairs to your deepest thoughts and feelings. Think about how amazing your relationship would be if there were no secrets and you were able to opening communicate, knowing that you would not be harshly persecuted by your spouse. Imagine a feeling of freedom and the ability to help each other grow as individuals. To have your spouse truly be your best friend, that you can share ANYTHING with.

Open communication takes away the guessing game. Has your spouse ever said something that shocked you and you thought, "I had no idea you thought that way?" Or you look up one day wondering who this person is because it's surely not the person you THOUGHT you married? Those are all signs that you all have not been having real conversations and someone has been changing over the years right under your roof and you had no idea. Uncut, blunt, and real conversations can have your marriage on the highest level possible. Take away communication and you can guarantee you marriage will wither because your sunshine (communication) no longer exists.

Our personal story.....

Growing up I (Candace) can't recall my parents having any arguments in my presence. My mother is soft spoken and has a meek spirit. As a little girl evidently I watched her and adopted that same concept. So when the storms were raging in my marriage I realized I would overtly bite my tongue for peace's sake. I didn't want to argue. (And I actually realized I took this path in other aspects of my life). In my mind, I wanted to avoid a confrontation at all costs. Therefore, I didn't address issues when I should have.

Then one day I faced a hard truth. I had been sacrificing my inner peace to keep the peace with others. There may have seemed to be outward peace, but I was wrestling with things in my mind that I should have said or done in these situations. So actually there was no peace! And with this being in the forefront of my mind, I stopped laying down and WOKE UP!! It took me noticing that not speaking up was not getting me a positive or peaceful outcome for me to decide to let my voice be heard, even if a disagreement or argument pursued. Not talking about it was not making the problem go away.

I should have opened up and discussed my expectations, wants, and needs with my husband. If I would have used my voice I could have prevented certain situations from reoccurring instead of being a mad mute when he did or didn't do something. Holding in my words and getting upset with my husband about things I had not clearly communicated to him was totally wrong on my part. How can we hold our spouse accountable for something they have no earthy idea about? That is ludicrous! It's not fair to your spouse or your marriage. We make the assumption that our spouse should "know" us and know everything we desire or dislike. We all know what they say about assumptions.

We were ten years into our marriage when I made a conscious decision to fully remove the muzzle (lol). It's time to be brutally honest and real. I'm not holding back anything I need to say because if I don't say it, my husband will not know. Verbalizing my concerns and wishes doesn't require me to disrespect or degrade my husband in any way.

By the way ladies, your delivery is everything. Depending on how you come at him, will determine if he listens with his heart or his head. I wanted true peace. I wanted my husband to know what was in my heart. I wanted our marriage to be real and that required me to improve on my communication skills.

WHY DO MEN GET IRRITATED WHEN A WOMAN SAYS, "WE NEED TO TALK!"?

RT: It's real simple...when you hear those four gut wrenching words MOST of the time it's about something WE (the man) have done or what WE NEED to do. We already know it's an issue with US. "We need to talk" is very rarely about Y'ALL tripping, mistreating us, or saying inappropriate crap. Those four words do not pertain to y'all correcting Y'ALL's BEHAVIOR!!!

CT: (Bursts out laughing)

RT: "We need to talk" automatically sends a message to our brain..."Awww man, what did I do now?", "Lord, Jesus what now", "What I do!" We get irritated because we know it's about our shortcomings. We know we did something and we don't want to HEAR IT.

CT: But what if it's not about something you did but something.....

RT: IT DON'T MATTER, that's what we are assuming. Y'all could very well want to discuss something other than us but that's what pops in our head.

CT: So we can't even begin the conversation on a positive note because y'all are already in defense mode.

RT: NOPE! We go into defense mode when we heard, "we need to talk". If you want to tick a man off INSTANTLY, say those words.

(We are both dying laughing at this point)

I've been with fellas that got a phone call or text when the girl was saying, "We need to talk." His attitude changed immediately. This is how it goes:

"DANG" (Deep groan)

"What, fool?"

"We need to talk."

"Huh?"

"That's what she just said, we need to talk."

"Awwww!!! Good luck, man." (Pat on shoulder.)

If it's a group of guys we are ALL hollering, "Aww. What you do, fool?" Men attitudes just change. I've seen dudes leave. They will try to stay and play it off for a second but you know you have to dip off somewhere. Or they choose not to call and just deal with it tomorrow.

CT: So ladies, now we know! Here is a golden nugget for you: Stop saying, "we need to talk" and just start talking. LOL. Don't give him an opportunity to become defensive before you can get the topic out.

CAN A LACK OF COMMUNICATION DESTROY A MARRIAGE?

RT: I believe it can. Without communication what can you have in a relationship? Communication covers a number of topics such as expectations, demands, wants, needs, desires, kids, and work. It's important to be able to come home, relax, and share the highs and lows of your day with your partner. Communication is the building block. If we cannot exchange in a verbal conversation about the things stated above what in the heck are we doing? We are simply co-existing. And when you and your spouse are not connected socially, you are guaranteed to be unhappy and less fulfilled within your union.

If you are going to communicate, especially for a man dealing with a woman, you have to be able to dialogue about anything to fulfill her needs. When there are certain topics you refuse to discuss you cause uncertainty and make her feel insecure in the life she shares with you. You better trust and believe she needs to communicate. It is just how women are wired. They need to talk while men can get by just fine without having to talk about EVERYTHING, in my opinion. Men, you need to be sensitive to that. It is impossible to have a successful marriage without communicating.

CT: Sometimes we women need to talk but are afraid to do so. The lack of communication will be the demise of any marriage. I thought discussing less would mean avoiding an argument. That was not healthy for me or our marriage. It caused unnecessary issues because I didn't communicate my needs or wants. It could be as simple as me needing a hug when I came home. If I haven't informed Remon of this and I'm getting upset because he has not given me this affection, it can confuse him.

When you are not talking to each other, you will find yourself discussing your problems with others. This is how people end up in the arms of others because someone took the time to be attentive and listen to a broken heart. Or you are conversing with friends about your problems, which may or may not provide healthy advice to feed your relationship. Seeking advice from your friends and/or telling them what you are feeling and going through instead of talking to your spouse is going against the grain. I will admit that your friends can give you information that will be helpful to your marriage. But, be careful with whom you wish to share your hurt and pain. If you choose to vent to others, make sure you also talk to the person that is actually involved (meaning your spouse) because they are truly the only ones who hold the true answers and responses you need.

Somebody Shoulda Told Me

Communication is not all always about talking. You also have to actively listen. Active listening means actually hearing your spouse's words and their heart. After your spouse has finished talking, you should be able to restate what you heard them say.

You cannot actively listen when you are gathering your thoughts in your head, ready for the comeback. The next time you all are in a dispute try this—after he/she finishes her point-of-view, say, "So what I hear you saying is..." This will allow you to show them you were actually paying attention and was present in the moment. Repeating what you heard will make sure what you internalized and processed is actually what they SAID and MEANT and that you did not allow your feelings and emotions to create a fictional story. How many times have you said something to later find out that your husband or wife HEARD something totally different? I know we can't be the only couple.

Communication needs to be important to you both. You cannot slack in this area. You have to be willing to talk even when you don't want to. Never go weeks without talking to each other. We know there will be times when you may need one, two, or maybe even three days depending on the severity. But the conversation must happen. The longer you go without interacting, the further you drift apart, and the easier it becomes not to care. Communicating should never be a door that is locked! Never lock your spouse out.

Somebody shoulda told you that men and women really do communicate differently. Well actually there are books that state this fact but I'm talking about real, in-your-face, present, people. My goodness, we speak two different languages!! And the crazy thing is you find yourselves arguing like two fools because you think the other one is saying something different and neither of you are actively listening. You have been arguing 30 minutes and at the point of being OVER IT. Then you calm down and discover you both have been saying the same thing just in "your" language. There is the man version and woman version...smh...lol.

Somebody Shoulda Told Me you are not going to always hear what you want to hear. It's not going to go your way all the time and it shouldn't. And guess what, that's all right. Your spouse might tell you something about yourself that you don't want to hear, but if you truly love one another and know it's coming from a loving heart, you have to be willing to listen and reflect on what he/she says. And self-correct if need be.

(We are NOT talking about accepting verbal abuse because that doesn't come from a loving heart.) When you say, "I Do" you should be marrying your best friend, so being willing and able to talk about anything is real love. The quality conversations that you are able to have with your closest friends and family should also apply to your spouse. In order to communicate on this level, it will take maturity, self-confidence, transparency, and a strong loving bond between both individuals.

Chapter 3

SEX

"Do not deprive each other except perhaps by mutual consent and for a time, so that you may devote yourselves to prayer. Then come together again so that Satan will not tempt you because of your lack of self-control." 1 Corinthians 7:5

We have jumped the broom and sex is approved by God! Men are thinking, "YES I can get sex every day, any time of the day I want! It's going to be a constant flow of love making." Women are just as excited but she doesn't realize he is thinking like that. Regardless, we are on the same page and the bedroom (and other parts of the house) are hot spots. You look forward to coming home and wrapping your arms around your baby/honey/teddy bear. Matter of fact, you have been thinking about what you plan to do to them all day, sending pictures and steaming hot text messages throughout the day. During this honeymoon stage, the theme song for your sex life is MY MISSION IS TO PLEASE YOOOOUUU! And then comes the babies, mommy duties, trials and tribulations, which takes you from the peak to the valley.

Our personal story......

Going into a marriage you don't realize certain things will affect your sex life. The kids. Your career. Your age. The intimacy within the marriage begins to slow down. You begin to lose your closeness and connection. The lack of sex may cause your spouse to venture back into their unmarried mindset and way of life and seek attention from someone other than you.

We started having issues in this area when our third child was born. Candace's desire for sex was not on the level with mine. Nowhere close to it. And my understanding about it was bad. I will admit I should not have been so demanding and irrational. Then it got to the point of her not trusting me due to prior situations and in her mind she felt I was being unfaithful. Therefore, she didn't want to have sex because that's what was flashing through her mind.

HOW DO YOU WORK IT OUT IF YOU ALL HAVE A DIFFERENT SEX DRIVE?

RT: COMPROMISE! That word there, MAN, it's so ever present in a successful marriage. There has to be a give and take in your marriage. If you had to break the word marriage down in a few words compromise will have to be one of those words.

Next, you have to communicate. Find out the reason your spouse is not as interested in intimacy. It may be something that you could be doing to hinder or help in this area. She might desire role playing, you might need to get back into shape or lose weight, or she may be overtired, over stressed and over worked. It could be medical or a hormone thing. The key is to find out what your spouse needs to feel connected to you sexually. Once you determine the issue, you must do your part to fix it, if you can.

ARE YOU REQUIRED TO HAVE SEX WITH YOUR HUSBAND/WIFE? REGARDLESS IF YOU WANT TO OR NOT.

CT: Speaking with other women, all their husbands think about is sex. Sex, Sex, Sex. When we did our Couple's Lounge events, we heard that some women believe it is a choice. That women should not have to feel obligated to have sex with her husband.

Allow me to speak from my own personal experience. The only times I don't want to have sex with you is when I'm mad, not bothered, but MAD. That mad when your body feels hot! (Ah-ha moment— that's where that cliché comes from.) For me sex is an intimate exchange of emotions and passion. I know one of your complaints was that I didn't initiate it and my sex drive is not as high as yours. I made a point to never say no even when I didn't want to (except for the times mentioned above). There were many times when I was "good" but I made love to you because I knew you needed it. So bottom line, women, we are obligated to have sex with our husband even when we are mad, no excuses. I must be honest, having sex when I'm mad is hard to do. I just can't. Well I probably could, if I could just switch my mindset into intimacy mode.

RT: SO ARE YOU JUSTIFYING BEING WRONG??!! Which doesn't make sense.

CT: You don't want to have sex either when you're mad!

RT: I'm telling you what you are sitting here doing. I'm just telling you what you just said Candace! On one hand you said you are required to and on the other hand you are not required.

CT: NO! I said I don't want to when I'm mad and I DON'T. Yes I feel like we are required to, but do I want to, no. Let me add this little tad-bit. Women are interested in sex and very well may start her day with the intentions of having nookie with her bookie that night but after being the first one up, getting kids ready for school, dropping kids off at school, working eight hours, picking the kids up, cooking, cleaning, and then getting everyone ready for bed, SHOOT she is tired. If that is the issue you all should discuss an alternative to night nookie. Be creative and have morning nookie or meet up during lunch time. Maybe the hubby can take on some of the afternoon/evening duties too. Compromise!

RT: Yes you are required to have sex! I think the spouse should be understanding of the other person's situation. You shouldn't be unrealistic. If you know your wife or husband is in bed with a 102 fever don't try to get you some. If you see them extremely tired and you want IT that night be willing to sacrifice it, if you can. Or help out. If you see your wife is tired then cook, clean, help with homework, or fold a load of clothes. Whatever it takes to take the load off her. Man, you want them to be able to relax so you can get some loving later. But the bottom line is that the Bible says the only time you sustain from sex is when you choose to fast. And then you are supposed to come back together so the devil will not be able to tempt you 1 Corinthians 7:5.

Somebody Shoulda Told Me

Somebody Should Told Me that regardless if you don't want to have sex because you are tired you need to muster us the energy and transform your mind into a happy place ready to please your spouse. And if you are disconnected from your spouse due to infidelity or disrespect, understand that it will be hard to conform to his/her desires to make love. But, the longer you are intimately separated the quicker you grow apart. And the space between you will allow the devil enough room to create mayhem in your marriage.

RT: As a man, somebody shoulda told me that I could help my wife get in the mood by making her workload at home a little lighter. Men you know we are thinking about "IT" all day. Looking forward to getting home! And then your wife comes in the house looking tired and you (I) immediately get upset. Instead of getting upset at the THOUGHT of not getting none, get up and help her. Start cooking, help the kids with their homework, clean up, DO SOMETHING. A woman's job doesn't stop when she comes home so men, this is the moment when you give a little to GET A LOT ;).

Somebody Shoulda Told Me to never stop the romance. Women enjoy foreplay. Take the time to get her in the mood. Every man should know what his woman likes and dislikes. You need to cater to what SHE finds enjoyable. Think about the things you did in the beginning to wine and dine her. It could be as simple as a back or foot massage. Or you could surprise her with a homemade candlelight dinner. Men, we have to stay away from the mindset of "you're my wife, you are supposed to." That is such a turn off to women.

CT: For my wives out there, somebody shoulda told me that men are constantly thinking about sex. Honey, they can't get enough. If you walk by the TV in something showing your figure...SEX. If you bend over to pick up a toy...SEX. If you rub up against him...SEX. If you are eating ice cream...SEX. The Kinsey Institute did a research that stated men think about sex every seven seconds which would be equivalent to more than 500 times an hour and more than 8,000 times during the approximately sixteen hours we are awake. Others later questioned this research's accuracy for numerous reasons. Other research has been done involving both men and women with significantly lower numbers. BUT yet, it still proves men think about sex double the number of times than most women. With that being said, wives even when you think this should hold him for a couple of days, he still wants it tomorrow, better yet he is ready for Round 2! Some men don't care if y'all are mad at each or if "Aunt Mary" is visiting. None of that stops the show. And some women are guilty of this because of their high sex drive.

Somebody Shoulda Told Me that men would like for their wife to initiate sex more often. Our husbands want to know that we want them just as much as they want us. They do not want to be the only one showing effort. Ladies, buy some lingerie. I know, I know it doesn't stay on longer than three minutes. That's okay, compromise. Men are visual creatures, so take the time to keep your "special drawer" stocked with lace and see-through pieces.

Chapter 4

INFIDELITY

"Marriage should be honored by all, and the marriage bed kept pure, for God will judge the adulterer and all the sexually immoral." Hebrews 13:4

The title of this chapter is Infidelity so of course we will deal with the big "C" word, CHEATING. Even though we have already talked about cheating, the fact that infidelity is the reason for 55% of the divorces warrants us to dedicate a chapter totally to this topic. Infidelity does to a marriage what an earthquake does to the earth. It shakes and destroys the foundation upon which you have built your relationship. And the pain pierces your heart and soul like a sharpened dagger. After experiencing infidelity, it takes time to rebuild and stop the bleeding from your heart. It's hard to love your spouse the way you used to. Those images that flash through your mind keep you in bondage with no chains.

Our personal story……

My wife and I faced this issue in our marriage but we have dealt with it and gotten past it. There were emails and inappropriate social media messaging as well. Infidelity is serious problem, at some point, in a lot of marriages destroys what the couple has built. It almost destroyed ours. While doing research for our book we discovered infidelity was always in the top five reasons for divorce in almost every source we found.

We found out there are many different types of cheating. So, in this chapter we will deal with—

- several causes for infidelity from his and her point of view.
- The struggles of getting past infidelity.
- The steps needed to get past infidelity.

As, most of you know men and woman both handle their spouse's cheating in different ways. I've heard women say men can never bounce back from cheating or it's nearly impossible. We will discuss why it is difficult for them. We then will dive into how you can bounce back even stronger than after cheating.

CT: Women can get over the hurt and pain quicker than most men. Men who are the victim of a cheating woman many times can't make it back to seeing their wives the same way, which ultimately leads to divorce. Those images and thoughts of her being with another man cloud his judgement. She was supposed to be his. Maybe not to her face, but he has called or thought of her as a whore because of it.

RT: After an affair both men and women are able to forgive and regain the pure image they had of each other. More men are forgiving their wives and I can't understand why we can't get our due diligence. Y'all are tripping. "Oh my wife cheated so it's over and I don't want to have anything else to do with her." That is the biggest false statement you can make. More men are staying. There are women who have cheated and realized, "I'm tripping, I'm about to lose a good dude and my family." She can get back on the straight and narrow. It's possible for both men and women to recommit to their marriage.

CT: Let me go back to my original statement about truly being able to forgive and move forward. I heard this and have experienced this next statement I'm about to make. Men DO NOT let sleeping dogs lie. Y'all will continue to bring stuff up from three decades ago. So if he took her back, you can bet your bottom dollar SHE WILL NEVER hear the end of it!! It will constantly be brought back up. He could have done it a million times to her one, but he just will not let it go (singing in my Frozen voice).

RT: But the difference between men and women, women want SAY it they will ACT it out. Instead of saying it, let a man do something that triggers her mind back to that state, she won't say one word but she will do something where he can tell she is pissed off! He won't have a clue that he just triggered her and sent her back to that place of hurt and betrayal when the incident happened or what she THOUGHT happened. She goes into shut down mode and becomes cold as ice.

CT: That is slightly accurate (winking eye). ALTHOUGH it does not happen for 5, 10, 20, 25, 30, 35, 40, 45, FIFTY YEARS! It doesn't transpire that long with women. Y'all just don't move on very well.

RT: So you said you have experienced this. Enlighten me!

CT: Yes I have and with you. I just don't feed into it nor do I acknowledge you stirring up old news. It could be true or false, if you have a thought about something you will continue to bring it up. And with us it wasn't related to cheating. For example, when we were in college your cousin told you he saw me on a Que's shoulder at the Texas Relays (which was not the truth). You brought that up for years, well into our marriage. The bad part is that you will bring up stuff that is not the truth. Then there are times when you keep asking me about a situation, unwilling to believe the answer I gave you the previous 100x's you asked, rotfl.

So again I stand firm on my view that men are unwilling to forgive like women.

RT: I promise if you get that same couple and ask that dude is there something your wife nags you about or keep bringing up, he will say yes. He may have caused it because he has done a lot more.

CT: Why do you think women are cheating?

RT: There is going to be a different reason for every woman.

CT: Let me speak for my ladies. When a woman says I do, she is all in. She is ready for a monogamous relationship with her friend, lover, and soulmate. But what seems to happen is he is still focused on others skirts which causes his time and energy to be taken off his wife and family. He stops being a team player. Men go from basketball player to tennis player. Meaning they go from being on a team to now being a single player. It's brings a great amount of pain to a woman's heart when she realizes she is not enough. To forgive one act of infidelity is bearable but to constantly discover your husband is spending time with other women or putting all the responsibilities on her, that causes her "marriage tunnel vision" to evaporate and her peripheral vision becomes keen. Her heart is hurting like a bad tooth ache and she is looking for a soothing medicine to take away the pain. That "medicine" can come in many forms but because we are people and need companionship, another man gives her the temporary relief she needs.

RT: I agree with you. And the sad part is we never have a clue that it's happening. If we find out we start to look back and identify certain things. The reason we don't have a clue is because we are so focused on "doing ME" and are not tuned into our wives. We are too busy doing our thing we never notice another man is doing what God purposed us to do for her as her husband.

Advice: It is possible that your wife is 100% faithful and has not given herself to another man nor interact with another man inappropriately. My advice to the brothers is to do your job and make sure your wife is happy. If we commit to our role to the best of our abilities and constantly try to improve as a husband if you have a good wife she will notice. If she cheats anyway that's on her. If she cheats when you're not a good husband, that's on her too. Is it possible to push her away, yes, but that's vice versa. And if we step out that's on us. Bottom line, it is possible to have a marriage free of infidelity.

CT: In your marriage 80% of the time everything will be good but that 20% is a bad boy! The 20% has a tendency to cause a temporary moment of amnesia about the good times. There is not a marriage or relationship on this side of heaven where 100% of your needs are met and you are overjoyed with that person all the time. Therefore, the 80% has to trump the 20%. I know that the 20% is a bad mama jama because it makes people chi-chi right into the arms of someone else. Most of the time they are simply seeking what they are not getting from their spouse. Just keeping it real. I know sometimes your marriage will be 60-40, 50-50, or even 20-80.

Regardless, infidelity is a choice. Anybody in any marriage can find an excuse to cheat, because no marriage is perfect. And since we don't live in a perfect world and no person is perfect, neither spouse is 100% efficient. Ladies, I do believe there are SOME men that can be faithful from the moment they say, "I do...until death do them part" (probably a man that gets married at 80 years old, rotfl). And for those that struggle initially with being faithful, I believe with God's intervening and his desire, a man can live a life committed to only one woman. He can shift his mindset, remembering why he married her, and decide to be satisfied with his beautiful wife.

Somebody Shoulda Told Me

Cheating does not carry a universal definition in a marriage. When entering a relationship or if currently married, it is important to discuss exactly what YOU consider cheating is because it's not restricted to having sex with another person. You must know what your spouse categorizes cheating as because you all could have different meanings. Also, somebody shoulda told me that you cannot allow your own assumptions and thoughts to become the reality of the situation. Your assumptions cannot convict your spouse before you hear the facts. You need to ask questions and move forward based on the facts. If you feel like the truth is not being told, you have the right to ask more questions but once you get to the point of moving on do so only with the evidence you have and what your spouse has admitted to.

Somebody Shoulda Told Me that a marriage can survive when infidelity has occurred. You must know that when your spouse cheats it is not your fault but their choice. You have to understand when someone cheats multiple times you will begin to wonder if you are good enough, does my spouse want to remain married, or is there something I can do to keep him/her satisfied. But it may have nothing to do with you and everything to do with him/her and where his/her head is.

If you are questioning whether it's worth it, you have to use your heart and head to judge if you want to remain in your marriage. Listening to one without the other leads to an imbalanced decision. Your heart checks with your emotions to see if they are alive and passionate about your boo. Your head looks at the reality of the situation and allows you to see things as they truly are. You must analyze several aspects when determining the future of your relationship: your emotional state, years married, children involved, number of times it has occurred, and the state of your marriage prior to the infidelity.

Somebody Shoulda Told Me that making the decision to remain in your marriage has to be solely on you. You may need a shoulder to cry on and a listening ear, but you shouldn't ask anyone, "What should I do?" To keep it real, you have to live with the decision you make so what someone else thinks is irrelevant. You can't listen to all that advice because when put in the same dilemma some people wouldn't follow their own darn counsel. Your peers have no idea about EVEYTHING that happens under your roof so they are making a one-sided judgement call with only half of the information.

Somebody Shoulda Told Me that once the act of infinitely has been brought to the surface, if you were unfaithful you must lay all the cards on the table. Straight shot, no chaser. You have to tell the whole truth, nothing but the truth, so help you God! God is who you are going to need if you try to lie your way through your explanation. The truth can eliminate doubts. Don't let your mind play tricks on you…making you believe reserving some of the details is protecting her/him. The deed is done. The pain is there. Tell everything at the beginning so the wound is not reopened as the truth comes out one layer at a time over days, weeks, months, or years. If you decide to move forward and not tell the whole truth, you'll discover how big a mistake it is later when your spouse finds out you lied. He or she will return back to the pain, topped with the pain of being betrayed once again. Mr. or Mrs. Cheater, please understand that a slew of questions are headed your way. Be prepared. Be understanding. Be truthful. FYI—please don't make the mistake of saying, "I don't want to talk about this" because you are going to make things go south real quick and possibly end your marriage.

Somebody Shoulda Told Me how to overcome infidelity:

1. Be honest.

2. Answer all the questions being asked.

3. Be genuine in your apology and acknowledge your wrong doing/Be willing to accept the apology.

4. Choose the right decision for you.

Chapter 5

FORGIVENESS

"For if you forgive other people when they sin against you, your heavenly Father will also forgive you. But if you do not forgive others their sins, your Father will not forgive your sins." Matthew 6:14-15

Forgiveness – to cease to feel resentment against someone that has offended you[1]. ~ Dictionary.com

Forgiving someone for hurting you is NOT easy, especially when they know "the act" would cause you pain if you discovered it. How selfish can we be to do something for our pleasure that could and would hurt the one we love?

Our personal story….

    It was hard for me to forgive Candace at a time when I felt like she was kicking me while I was down. I held on to the pain for many years and it affected our marriage in several ways. I viewed her as my opponent instead of my teammate. My pain turned into anger and I released it into the atmosphere of our home, our marriage, and in my

---

[1] http://dictionary.reference.com/

actions towards her. The pain took over my mindset and I was unwilling to forgive her. After going through our few sessions of counseling, I realized that holding onto the hurt I felt was not only hurting her but it was hurting us. And although I wanted to hurt her--not physically of course--I was unconsciously hurting myself because she began to lash out at me. I knew in order for our marriage to grow I had to decide to start telling myself a new story, a positive one. I had to stop living in the past because it was not beneficial to our future. My love for Candace and my family outweighed my desire to hold steadfast in my pain. Staying married to the love of my life was more valuable.

    The first time you experience a situation that requires forgiveness it feels like you are being suffocated by the pain. It is hard to forgive at first because of the whirlwind of emotions...shock, confusion, hurt, pain, and disbelief. Trying to process those feelings on top of dealing with the situation is like standing in quicksand...the more you struggle in your thoughts the faster you sink into depression, unhappiness, and/or rage.

    OMG! If you don't discuss the situation you will start creating short stories in your mind. You create the setting, characters, the plot, etc. Driving yourself straight crazy, trying to figure out the puzzle.

    When you are spiritually connected to God, you know it is His command that we forgive others. But the flesh will make you become irrational at times. Being willing to forgive is a non-negotiable in order to move forward in your relationship. It comes down to a choice— you choose to stay or leave.

    Forgiveness is not for the person, but for you. When you choose not to forgive you are carrying unnecessary bricks of weight with you daily. You can wear a fake mask of happiness to cover up your true emotions, but your soul is decaying every second of the day you choose to hold on to the pain and anger. Not only do you have to be willing to forgive others, you also have to be willing to forgive yourself.

Forgiveness is something we both had to do, and something we both struggled with doing when the time presented itself. What we mean by struggle is that it was hard to get pass it. It all depends on what you are forgiving them for. The need to forgive your spouse may come within the first six months of your marriage, if not you better believe it will happen within the first year. It could be as simple as saying something in the heat of a moment, being inconsiderate, or forgetting a birthday.

You have to express the emotions that you feel when they hurt you. If you are not comfortable expressing yourself in the privacy of your home or if you feel like there will be no resolution if you do, consult a professional or a neutral third party.

When you are unwilling to open your heart to forgive them ask yourself, "Why am I choosing to hold on to this pain/anger?" Yes, there will be many times in your relationship that will cause you to self-reflect. Figuring out why can allow a break through that could save your marriage.

CAN YOU FORGIVE AFTER BEING TRULY HURT?

RT: Yes! People do it all the time. I've seen and talked to people who were sure they'd lost their marriage, lost their husband or wife. It was a wrap! Then they got to a point of forgiveness and their relationship is better than it was before. Is it difficult, yep.

CT: I believe when you have been hurt to your core, when you can literally feel the pain beating in harmony with your heart, it is harder and the recovery process is even more difficult. Forgiveness requires you to shift your mindset...you may not forget the incident(s) but you have to forget the pain it caused you in order for you to move forward with or without that person.

RT: Ok, I can feel that.

CT: You have to look at that person as the person you fell in love with. Of course this is for isolated incidents. Abuse is a whole 'nother ball game. But the person that caused the hurt and pain must realize forgiveness is a process. And let me define process for those who believe it can or should happen in a few days. A process is defined as a SERIES of actions or steps taken in order to achieve a particular end. And let me go ahead and define series: a number of things or events that are arranged or happen one after the other. Therefore, everyone's "process" will be different and require different things to occur.

RT: Yeah, you are correct. You have to know you are about to go through a little hell from your wife (husband). You are not about to get too many happy faces or long conversations. Matter of fact, I'm sure she is shooting you several side-eyes and turned-up lips. You better believe you are going through some: YOU HURT ME, I'M PISSED OFF DON'T TALK TO ME, and YOU SURELY BETTER NOT THINK ABOUT TOUCHING ME. But the odd thing is you realize you caused the hurt and pain yet you have a problem going through the human grinder. Oh man, the wrath that comes with hurting someone! I know because I'm guilty of it. You are not truly grasping, at the time, how you hurt your spouse. And you are like, "Man it's been a day, two days, MAN she still tripping!" But you do not understand how hurt she really is. So both people have to be careful because you don't want to stay mad, bitter, and angry so long that it robs you of your joy. There are some people that can't get pass the hurtful act and I can't fault them. But don't beat them down forever because of this mistake. Allow yourself to grieve and take your time, but you have to move past it for your marriage to survive.

CT: I want to say to all the women, don't intentionally try to stay mad just so he can get a taste of the pain he caused you. I believe there is a natural emotion and reaction to being hurt and I know we can intentionally keep it going for the sake of hurting him. How do I know? Because I've done it before. I chose to stay mad well beyond my natural emotional reaction. Let's call it what it is, revenge. At that time in our marriage, I felt as if he didn't care about my wants, needs, or feelings. He was not providing me the security or love I felt I needed and my feelings were hurt. I couldn't understand why he just didn't get it. I made a conscious decision to put on a mad persona whenever I was in his presence. I could be laughing and playing with my kids, just come back from GNO (Goddess Night Out), or been having a heck of a good time with my family BUT with him, NOT! Okay, let me get back to the topic at hand-- forgiveness. It put so much darn stress on me to maintain my new "acting" role, which really wasn't worth it. It was not beneficial to our marriage at all. So if it only takes you a couple of days to get over it, then let it go. Talk to your husband (wife) and resolve the issue.

RT: I also think it depends on the severity of the incident. This will definitely dictate some things (chuckle) especially the process and the timeline. You can easily forgive someone coming home late but forgiving infidelity is going to take some time.

CT: PREACH!

RT: Especially if you get busted red-handed and you have done it several times.

CT: Well let's take this conversation a little further. Has one really forgiven if you keep bringing up the incident?

RT: Yes, I think so. (Deep breath) I can see how it could be perceived not to be forgiven if you keep bringing it up. I think depending on the situation, either the person has not forgiven, wants or needs closure, may still be hurt, mayyybbee....what else could it be?

CT: (LOL)

RT: I don't know, OR JUST TRIPPING (lol). I think a person can forgive, yet still bring it up. And maybe that's not how you should go about it but because a person brings up something does not mean they have not forgiven. Well, let me say that you should not do it. If you have forgiven your wife (husband), let it go. So Candace you believe if a person keeps bringing up the situation they have not actually forgiven that person?

CT: My opinion is this...if you are bringing it up constantly, meaning several times in a short duration of time, you have not really forgiven them. Especially when it's brought up at an irrelevant time, i.e. throwing a jab or a "hot one". Now if you are talking about the subject and you want to make a valid point that maybe a little different and it is possible.

    Let me give you an example: After an incident of infidelity they leave for a few days or you decide to separate, then you decide to take them back. You tell them you forgive them yet you take them back down memory lane, frequently, then you have not truly forgiven them. And you must be honest with yourself and look within to determine what is blocking you from shifting your mind.

ARE WOMEN MORE LIKELY TO FORGIVE THE ACT OF INFIDELTY THAN MEN?
(Ladies we already know the answer but let's be entertained)

CT: I will lead this one off sir. I know for a fact women are more forgiving and understanding when it comes to cheating. Although I'm not quite sure why. Could it be society? We live in a society where women think all men cheat so if you leave for that reason you better realize you will never be in a relationship. That actually makes sense seeing that 70% of married men commit adultery. Although that may be the case I'm going to assume women are more forgiving because our hearts are bigger, our minds are sharper, and our soul exuberates a strong connection to the man we love. Let me say this: Regardless of what society wants us to believe or accept, God says in the Ten Commandment, *Thou shall not commit adultery*. (Exodus 20:14 KJV) Therefore a husband being faithful to his wife is EXPECTED. I believe any and every man is capable of being faithful to his wife.

RT: I think women are probably leading in that statistic but please believe that gap is closing. Men are more forgiving these days than ever before. Maybe the fact that more men in church these days with a closer relationship with God is the reason there has been a shift in our mindset. I tell you women are cheating and men are forgiving. Dudes are forgiving more, and more, and more than ever before. Take a look around. Women are out here cheating. Women probably have a lead in the forgiveness aspect but that lead is NOT how it use to be by no shape, form, fashion, or any way you want to look at it.

CT: Married women???

RT: Yes! That's who this book is talking about ain't it?! Married women and men.

CT: So, tell me why is it harder for men to forgive? I'm definitely not condoning or promoting adultery but we both know it does exist in most marriages.

RT: I believe most men don't think their wife will cheat but the reality is some women will. Men just can't deal with it.

CT: I think it's deeper than that.

RT: I'm speaking from MY opinion. That's the main reason and they just can't get past it. POINT BLANK! She did it and I can't see myself with her from this day forward. I'm out!

Somebody Shoulda Told Me

Matthew 6:14-15 says, *"For if you forgive other people when they sin against you, your heavenly Father will also forgive you. But if you do not forgive others their sins, your Father will not forgive your sins."*

We all need to post this somewhere in our home for a reminder and quick reference. Somebody shoulda told me that we must be willing to forgive because we are not perfect and both parties will make mistakes. Forgiveness does not mean you have to remain in your marriage/relationship. You can mutually decide to part ways but you have to free your heart from resentment.

Somebody Shoulda Told Me to be present in your marriage at all times. You should be able to identify your spouse's weaknesses and strengths as an individual and recognize how both affect your marriage. More than likely their weak areas are where they will make the mistakes that need to be addressed. If you are not willing to forgive, you will not have a happy marriage. You have to be willing to move past it as quickly as you can because being unwilling to forgive will have a domino effect that will cause your whole house to collapse.

How Do You Forgive?

1. Stop being in shock! Realize and accept that it happened.

2. Sit down and talk about it. The accused needs to explain why they did it. The victim has the right to ask ANY and EVERY question they want answered. This is when both parties need to be open and honest about their feelings. Neither spouse should make the statement, "You shouldn't feel like that." Allow them to speak their truth

3. If forgiving them is still difficult, ask yourself what is causing you to hold on to the pain. Why are you making this choice? If you have a growth mindset, you should have an ah-ha moment.

Forgiveness allows the healing process to begin. And until this comes to fruition, you will maneuver about life with an open wound that is exposed and subject to "infection". Arguments, dishonesty, misunderstanding, reoccurring acts of anything you don't like enters that wound as bacteria which continue to eat away at your body, soul, and mind.

Chapter 6

COMPROMISE

"Wives, submit yourselves to your own husbands as you do to the Lord." Ephesians 5:22

"Husbands, love your wives, just as Christ loved the church and gave himself up for her."
Ephesians 5:25

Compromise – an agreement or a settlement of a dispute that is reached by each side making concessions[2]. ~Oxford Dictionaries

As you go into a marriage this is just another component that you will need to think about and realize you will HAVE to do. Getting married at 25 years of age, I hadn't yet faced the type of disputes that I would become a part of as a married woman. When you are single, you only have to compromise with yourself. You come and go as you please, shop as you please, make decisions regarding your person as you please. That all changes once you decide to

---

[2] http://www.oxforddictionaries.com/us

wear a ring purchased by another person, and for a woman, take the name of her husband.

Compromising will more than likely start the first week of marriage if not the first day after the "I do's". It is vital because it creates a balance within your union. If your spouse is "all about me", take, take, taking, it will leave you feeling invaluable and unfulfilled. If you are the one who has to give in all the time you will become stifled in your personal growth as well as in the marriage.

Not compromising is how people "lose" themselves once they get married. By the way, deciding to get married does not require you to become less important nor forgotten about.

Our personal story....

Remon smoked a tobacco product that he was addicted to. I could not stand the smell of it and did not want it in my presence. The fact that he was "addicted" to this product irritated the Sam Hill out of me. I requested that he not smoke in the house and my car. Not only did I not want him smoking in my car but I asked him not to smoke in his truck if I was with him. Initially, he felt like it was his vehicle and I had no right to make that request. It was his right and privilege to do as he pleased in his truck. Let's just say there were many arguments every time he lit one up with me in this closed environment. He finally gave in to how much it bothered me and was willing to compromise his desire to smoke in order for me to be healthy and happy.

When you are young, you really don't know what it truly means to have to compromise with another grown person regarding affairs that may or may not affect them directly. It is our human nature to want what we want. This mentality begins at birth and it never goes away. It doesn't matter what age we are, there are always times when we feel a sense of entitlement.

Therefore, you don't grasp the things you will have to compromise on or why you should even have to compromise at all. Even if someone explains it to you, it may be difficult for your mind to comprehend why you would have to compromise on certain things. I (Candace) do not understand why someone would have to compromise when the issue is regarding their person i.e. a certain hairstyle, choosing to wear make-up, clothing style, etc.

Compromising is very difficult when you are in a stage where you don't like each other. When your marriage is in the valley, very little compromising is probably going on. Heck, you probably ain't even talking to each other therefore you are making decisions and could care less what your spouse thinks about it. (Can we say we have been there?)

Overall, compromising has never been a real issue for us. Now we are not saying we didn't dispute, but one of us was willing to give in, or better yet, agree in order to make things happen. I would charge that to our personalities. We are opposites in many areas so we balance each other out. I'm a busy body and he is more chilled. I eat a variety of foods and he is more selective. I'm a big dreamer and he goes with the flow. Then there are areas where we are a lot alike…he loves sports and so do I, he likes to have fun and so do I, we worship in the same religion, just to name a few. Even so, we have had a few arguments where we went round and round and round before someone through in the towel.

WHEN COMPROMISING, DOES IT REQUIRE YOU TO COMPROMISE YOUR HAPPINESS?

CT: I do not believe so. When a situation is being debated, first and foremost you have to get clarity of the other person's point of view. When you don't agree, both people should be able to state their position, rationally explaining what they want as their spouse listens. If your reason is justifiable or valid, than I should be willing to give in. And because I love you, and this decision will bring you happiness, I should be elated also (in our marriage, seeing compromise at this level has just become clear to us).

For example, we are currently looking for a new home. I want four bedrooms, two bathrooms, two living areas, a large master bedroom, plus an office space is MANDATORY. You want the same except for an office space, so you don't feel like that should be a deal breaker. You would rather have a man cave/game room. So as we have searched for our home we can't seem to find a house that has all our needs plus our wants (office and man cave). Well at least not in our price range.

As we continue to look, what if we find one that has the four bed-two bath, open floor plan, office space but no game room? So therefore other than the game room, it's everything we could ask for. We could opt out and decide that since we can't find one with both an office and game room we will sacrifice and just choose a house that has neither, so we both do without. It's neutral, and it's a lose-lose situation for us both. OR we can sit down and negotiate...lol. I can state the reasons I NEED an office: a place of peace to be creative, organize and implement my goals, manage my business endeavors, read for personal growth, and be my War Room. Then you realize you want a man cave as a place to invite your boys over and watch sports, have a few drinks, and do man stuff or just a place for you to escape to have me-time. After thinking about the two, you decide to compromise and allow me to purchase a home with an office space instead because you can always ask us to leave and invite your friends over and do all that in the family room. Plus you realize we can both benefit from the office space. You are not bitter about the decisions but actually happy because you were able and willing to see me happy although you didn't get exactly what you wanted. And when mama is happy she will make sure you are happy. Let me go to the "special" drawer. Therefore, you have not compromised your "happiness" because you are happy because I am. And folks THAT'S LOVE.

RT: In certain situations I believe compromising will cause you to be unhappy. But for the most part I agree with you. So here is a situation when I think you can be unhappy when you have to compromise. Say for instance I have a homeboy you don't think I should be hanging with and you come to me and say, "I don't like him or what he is about. He has loose morals and he seems to forget you are a married man. So you need to reconsider hanging out with him." A man may not like the idea of not being able to hang with his boy. But in a marriage, if your wife hits you with this man you might just have to compromise that relationship for the sake of your marriage.

Now if you have a husband or wife who is jealous and they don't want you hanging with anyone or find an issue with everyone, THEY need to look within and find out what is making them so insecure. It can't be something wrong with everybody. If your spouse is not this type of person you will need to think long and hard about it because this will be difficult to do. If you tell her that you will stop hanging with him, you are going to have to actually do it because if you say one thing and do another it's not going to be pretty when she finds out. If she is bothered by this person that much, as your Queen you will have to honor her request. Any man....(interrupted)

CT: But you would be unhappy by granting my request in this situation? (As I sit and type this now I think I would be more confused and upset if he made this request of me—which is being unhappy so I guess there are certain situations BUT because we recorded this long conservation I will add it in the book).

RT: No. I don't think in that situation I would really be unhappy.

CT: Wait. You are supposed to be giving me an answer to support your point-of-view.

RT: Well, maybe that was a bad example. Let me think….Naw I'm going to take that back, yeah that's the situation I'm going to use! And not only could it be a friend but it could also be family.

CT: Oh no…not hanging with family is totally different! We can stop that thought 'ret now.

I just thought up a time to support your argument. It would be the first time we decided to not celebrate with my family on New Year's Eve. Oh, I was so mad that you decided you wanted to bring in the New Year in Dallas with your friends at that party. I ABSOLUTELY DID NOT WANT TO GO WITH YOU! I wanted to be with my family at my sister's party. I did compromise and was very unhappy, the entire night. I didn't even have a good time but I acted like it. Remember I sent them a GroupMe message when we returned to the hotel saying, "I miss yall and wish I was there". I was present physically but mentally I was with them.

RT: Dang, I didn't know that. You were THAT unhappy to go??!!

CT: Yes. As I think about it now—we were rebuilding our relationship at that time. Matter of fact, the summer of 2013 is when you really almost lost me. So being that it was only five months later, I had not recommitted my heart or spirit with you. But where we are today, more in love than ever before, valuing each other, working as a team, living each day to make the other one happy, communicating much better, operating with a totally different mindset....it doesn't matter where I am as long as I'm with you. And in that I find happiness.

So, compromising can cause you to be unhappy when you are not mentally and physically connected to each other. When you are not clicking on all cylinders, shoot the simplest request could tick you off.

RT: So you don't agree with me in saying certain situations, even if y'all are good can make you unhappy? That's a lie.

CT: I'm saying it depends on your current mindset in your marriage and how you view your spouse at that time.

RT: I got that! I can't argue with that. My daddy once told me, "Son, in your marriage it's going to come a time when one of y'all will not be in love with the other one. You will fall out of love. Just hope and pray it's not at the same time! And that the other one uses good judgement in the meantime."

CT: That statement is so real. I'm ecstatic that right now we have shifted into a higher dimension in our relationship. Our marriage is even better than when we first got married and was in that honeymoon stage. We got some "grown folks with experience" love going on. It feels different than ever before. To be real, I might not be a happy camper for a brief moment because I didn't get my way but I would be happy because you are.

RT: And truth be told, we both are going to have to compromise a great deal.

CT: Yep. If I compromise for you and you compromise for me, we should be happy because we giving a little and getting a little. It shows that we know how to work together. And when both people are compromising, no one should lose themselves in the marriage.

(Because of my last statement another discussion was started.)

RT: You should not lose yourself ONLY if "yourself" is benefiting the marriage. Some people NEED to be a whole other person for the marriage to work because if some people be "themselves"…that marriage ain't gon' work. You've got to be somebody else as a wife or husband. So be careful when you make THAT statement.

CT: (LOL) You are crazy…When I make mention of losing yourself I'm talking about giving up hobbies, having me time, putting your dreams on hold, etc. And this relates more so to women. Women/Mothers/Wives are so busy making sure everyone else is good they tend to forget about themselves. Women become so consumed with pleasing their husbands, raising their kids, taking care of the home, working to help provide that they guilty for stepping away for a moment to take care themselves. Before they know it, years have passed and they find themselves looking in the mirror and asking, "What happened?"

RT: Well, here is another statement I disagree with. "Some women lose themselves because they are so engulfed in their family, kids, and marriage". You are supposed to be!!

CT: NO YOU'RE NOT!

RT: OH, MY GOODNESS! For your family, you give up "I" for "we". Your family comes before your wants and needs. To think otherwise is not going into or continuing in your marriage correctly. If your home is completely unhappy because you don't want to lose yourself and compromise, you are wrong. To postpone your goals is not losing yourself. If you are in a healthy marriage your spouse will understand that you need a day or outing to do you. But that goes back to compromising like we discussed earlier. If your passion is taking away time from home, you might have to let it go but that's not losing yourself. But to you, it is and that baffles me.

CT: When I refer to losing yourself, there should not be an extended period of time, heck 30 days is too long, where you can't do something for yourself. If you manage your time properly nobody has to give up their dreams, passions, GNO's, hobbies, etc. Yes, your family comes first so if I wanted to do something but my kids had an event as well I'm not going to make them miss it because I want to do something. It's called prioritizing what needs to be done. Everyone in the home should be chasing goals and dreams they want to obtain, simultaneously. It always seems that people get a better understanding when you use their reality in a situation so check this out.

Remon you love the time you spend in the gym. It's your second home. What if I said the time you are spending working out, something you are passionate about, is taking away from the time you could be spending with your family and the money you're spending could be invested somewhere else. If I took that away from you, there would be a piece of your happiness gone. The gym is a big part of you and something you have enjoyed since the first day we met, actually since high school. You should not have to lose that part of your life, and as your wife, I know how much you love working out so for me to request you give it up is inconsiderate. It's absolutely no reason you couldn't simply adjust the time you went in order to accommodate my desire to have you at home to help me in the evening. This is a means to doing what you want without it affecting your family. I think a couple should work it out so no one feels a since of being "lost".

This doesn't mean you won't have to sacrifice at times. I feel losing yourself happens over a period of time when you are not taking care of yourself or neglect your wants, needs, and desires. So, you may have to give up a situation but never yourself. But this is just my opinion. To each his/her own.

RT: Baby, you have to give up ME for US. When it's all about us it works. You are on some extreme stuff. What you are saying is just too extreme for me.

CT: It's NOT extreme because there are women who do it every day! She puts her wants and needs on the back burner for everyone else. This is not "extreme", its reality. This just proves to me that men really don't realize how y'all wives may feel lost and no longer able to recognize the woman she has become while married to you.

Y'all don't grasp how tired and wore down she may be because she can't find time in her busy life to re-energize herself. Y'all don't have a clue. And the thing about it is, when she is not operating at her best, she can't be the best wife she can be or the best mother she could be.

RT: That's a personal issue on her part. And if she is doing everything for her kids and husband I'm not downing her for that. Matter of fact, I'm going to applaud this woman.

CT: So in that equation, she should not include herself because you sure didn't.

RT: I didn't say that. You can do things for yourself AND do things for your family.

CT: THAT'S—ALL—I'M--SAYING! That's exactly what I've been saying for the last twenty minutes, man. (Y'all see this is why communicating and getting an understanding is so important, goodness gracious. Lord help us.)

Then he had the nerve to say, "Some people go up, over, and around the hill to get to the point instead of taking a straight path. You went up, over, and around."

No sir that would be you.

Somebody Shoulda Told Me

Compromising, the most effective way, will require you to have a mature mindset. Please understand that compromising is more difficult when your marriage is being held hostage by hurt, anger, and unhappiness. So if any of these exist, it is important to communicate to discover the root of the issue so that you can maintain a sense of happiness in your relationship. When you compromise remember you are making your husband or wife happy. Both parties have to be willing to give a little so that you can have balance. When you find yourselves in a disagreement and a decision has to be made, sit down and calmly state your point-of-view.

Ladies, realize it will not always go our way. And fellas, although we have the final say, listen to your wife because God gave us her to bring wisdom. As a man, you should want to compromise to make your Queen happy. Couples have to view everything from two perspectives, theirs and their spouses. Love your spouse enough to be happy in seeing them happy even when things don't go your way.

Chapter 7
FINANCE

"Marriage is a partnership, and couples can't win with money unless they're doing the budget as a team." - Dave Ramsey

Finances are one of the top reasons for divorce. The lack of money brings on stress whether you are married, single, black, white, young, or old. But when you are married, unless otherwise stated, it's expected that both parties have an income. Most homes function off two sources of income. Couples are business owners of their home, and when you work together your home is successful. If someone stops contributing your home, your relationship has a high chance of failing. Let's say the lack of funds is due to a job loss or not making the desired amount. The person whom this is directly affecting may be very much stressed. Their spouse becomes stressed from having to deal with the other's attitude and mood swings, and withdrawal on top of their own emotions. Two people under the same roof experiencing high levels of anxiety makes a wild fire that can ignite at any moment if there is no attempt to handle the circumstances as a team, united, together we stand divided you will fall. Most people want to live the best life possible. Therefore, when obtaining the bare necessities are in jeopardy, you tend to venture into fight or flight mode.

Our personal story…

CT: You see when we got married, we were both college graduates so being financially unsure never entered our mind. We were both entering the educational field where jobs were plentiful. I'm sure we briefly mentioned finances in marriage counseling but it must not have been significant because we didn't recall any of it through the storms in our marriage. So we were novices on how finances could destroy our marriage. **SOMEBODY SHOULDA TOLD US!!**

After just one year of marriage, Remon was among a group of teachers that were surplussed from his first teaching job. He took a low paying job for the next school year. At this time our second child was born. Two years later, I started the school year with no teaching job and was forced to quit my side hustle at an upscale department store (that I had worked for the past three years while teaching) to take a full time job working as a daggum cashier at a home improvement store. What I discovered years later is that God used my career to grow me and bring me closer to Him, but that's a whole other story. The biggest financial breakdown that rocked our marriage to its core was when my husband had not gotten certified and was without a teaching job for approximately three years. Within these three years there were times he didn't have a job at all. Being without a job, he was dealing with his own emotions of not being able to provide and not feeling like the man of the house.

As for me, I was supportive initially but as months turned into years my frustration grew. My frustrations came from me not believing he was willing to do what needed to be done for his family, dealing with his attitude and mood swings. That frustration turned into anger. I felt as if he was not fulfilling his role as my husband nor as a father. I didn't feel secure, safe, or loved at this time.

Our biblical order was out of alignment. According to God, the order of the home is God, man, women, and then kids. What I realized years later when we were in our healing stages, is that because we had switched God's order and now I was the provider, security blanket, and leader, the switch caused all kinds of chaos to enter our marriage and home. Chaos showed UP and showed OUT! The lack of finances opened the door for so many other problems that after ten years of marriage we considered divorce for the first time. We had never even spoken the word to each other up until then.

Some women lose respect for their husbands in these situations. This is not an immediate reaction, but these feelings can develop over an extended period of time. Finances can be a thermostat in a marriage. When the finances are low, the love is cold. No emotions. If money is not an issue, it can be hot and heated. Having a financial discussion prior to marriage can defuse a lot of unnecessary clashing of the Titans. It has been statistically proven that financial strife can destroy a marriage. It's amazing how our great-grandparents, grandparents, and possibly even our parent's finances were not the best but they were able to stand the test during their time.

ARE WOMEN NOT ABLE TO HANDLE THEIR HUSBANDS NOT WORKING OVER A PERIOD OF TIME?

RT: I think a perfect saying comes from Ronnie Coleman, the body builder from Arlington, TX. "Everyone want to be big, but they don't want to lift no heavy weight." I said that to say this, if you are a woman or man and you are going through a financial crisis, and you have to carry the load, realize you got married for better or worse. I know some are a whole lot worse than others but you made a vow. If you are that unhappy you need to leave. But if you choose to stay and you have to lift that heavy weight…THAT'S MARRIAGE. **SOMEBODY SHOULDA TOLD YA!**

There will be times when the scale is tilted and you have to bear the burden of carrying the load at that particular time. In a marriage there will be several occasions when things are not equal, one person is doing more than the other person. If a woman has to be the bread winner for a period of time, she does not deserve brownie points for ensuring her house remains a home. Just like a man doesn't get brownie points for doing what he is supposed to do. If your spouse can't but you can, you are suppose too. Let's be clear, we are referring to men that are down on their luck and can't find a job at that time or not making what he would desire. We are NOT talking about men that sit at home, banging on a game system, smoking weed, or chilling on the couch all day.

As we discuss this topic, I can reminisce on a conversation I had with a friend. We were discussing how at one time we couldn't pay to take our wives to a concert but times had changed for the better. Long story short he said, "Never let your woman have to do more than you. If she does, you may never recover from it. I will never forget some of the stuff my wife said to me. Never let a woman have to do that!" Some women fold under that kind of pressure. They stand strong only for a while. In marriage you have the 80-20 rule. So if he is at 20 and you decided to stay in your marriage, carrying the load is what you will have to do for the moment.

SHOULD YOU KEEP YOUR MONEY TOGETHER OR IS IT BEST TO HAVE SEPARATE BANK ACCOUNTS?

CT: This was an actual discussion we had, in detail, prior to marriage. I wanted to do what my parents did, one account for bills and our own individual account. You said we should do it like your parents and put all our money together. You felt having separate accounts was creating a division from the start. We decided to have one account. Well everyone, I must tell you that DID NOT work for us at all! After several overdraft fees, I suggested we get our own account and do everything separately. FYI: this was during the time we begin to operate as two, instead of one, in our marriage. We didn't have any of our money together and each person was responsible for certain bills they were required to pay. Before beginning this book we decided to go back to a one-for-all for bills, kids and savings. I do feel that having our funds apart created an invisible divided line within our marriage.

RT: I think the bottom line is being on the same page. If you are on the same page, with one goal, having one bank account is very doable. I do believe in having separate accounts as well. You can have both. Your personal account is for you to go shopping, personal upkeep, hanging with your friends, etc. If you are financially stable there is going to be extra. First you need to make sure bills are paid, you have put some money in your savings account, tithes are paid, and kids are taken care of. Everything else is spare change. And if you are blessed to have some "play" money it's okay to have that money in a separate account. But to each its own. The key is to communicate and agree on how your marriage finances will be managed. Keep the dialogue going until you reach an agreement that you both are happy with and are willing to abide by. God is first, family second, and your individual wants and desires are last. You must sacrifice you for home when you are married but like I said earlier, if home is taking care of...DO YOU! One accord. One goal. Same page.

CT: But can you be on one accord by having a mindset of this is my money and that is your money?

RT: I'm sure there are two people doing it like that as we speak. I just think that's the wrong mindset. When you are thinking in such a manner you are more me-centered when the family is not. The family unit is not about me. It's about us, the unit.

WILL AN ISSUE ARISE IF THE WIFE MAKES MORE MONEY THAN HER HUSBAND?

CT: Although marriages have made new strides and the normal traditions of having roles in a marriage have dissolved a lot, I still see this as an issue for marriages.

RT: I don't! Well I do believe it is for women. I think more women get on a power trip or lose respect for their husband/boyfriend when she makes more. If she is a professional making a certain amount of money and this dude is making pennies, it's an issue. Let's say for instance, she is an executive making $75,000 a year and he is a bus driver making $30,000. That woman is going to have an issue with that. But flip the coin and watch a man that's an executive date a secretary with no problem. And marry her. Most women ain't trying to hear that at all! That's just my opinion because I see it over and over again.

CT: Well let me give my two cents...I'm not looking at this question from a dating perspective. If I were, I think when that woman went into the relationship knowing he was a bus driver it would not be a problem for her.

RT: But going into a relationship, women are not trying to date a man making a significant lower income than she is BUT a man will. A woman will not even look your way if you are not on her level. If you are not eating at THIS restaurant, driving THIS car, living in THIS house, she is in not even entertaining the idea of dating you. Women are NOT trying to hear it. Therefore, it is more of an issue with y'all.

CT: I agree with that in the dating realm. This question was derived from a marriage perspective.

RT: I still think it's more of an issue for women.

CT: Disagree! I believe a man's self-esteem and pride is eaten up like wood with termites on it if his woman makes a significant amount more than he does. I think it goes back to being the leader and provider of the home. He knows being the leader and provider is his God-given role and, because finances are a major factor of supporting the family, not all men are comfortable with the woman leading in that area. My thought is that it is an inner struggle for him and some men are so frustrated by it that it pours out into their marriage so they tend to lash out at their wife.

RT: I don't think that's the case anymore.

CT: DISAGREE...lol

RT: What make you think that way?

CT: I just believe the inner struggle is more real for a man.

RT: Well if that's the case the woman having an issue with her husband not equal to or above her income is more outwardly expressed. "Oh, I'm the boss NOW!", "I can do this now because I'm making more money."

CT: (bahahaha) She will not act like that if her husband is following his dreams and his career choice doesn't come with a high salary amount.

RT: Nope. You are wrong. PLEASE! I don't understand what you are saying here. If it's all one pot why would he trip with her?

CT: *(Maybe we should agree to disagree on this question. Sometimes that is a choice you have to make. You will not agree on everything and once you realize that it's time to move on...next subject. Yet we continue this conversation.)*

CT: He may not intentionally become argumentative with her but his inner frustration and thoughts will show up eventually. That's when women find themselves saying, "Where did that come from?" Y'all be on one and don't even realize it. Or maybe y'all do.

RT: Man, I know dudes that are in this situation and they don't care about their wife making more money. It's all coming home to the same pot. I'm doing what I enjoy and providing and she is doing what she likes. Why would he say, "Aww she making more money than me" (in a sad voice). I can see dudes feeling bad if they are not in their career field of choice or living in their purpose. And maybe he is unhappy with his life and his wife is thriving and doing well. In that situation I can see some dudes having an issue.

CT: (I swear we say the same things just in different languages. Jesus take the wheel. I've been saying that the whole time.) How about you take a poll from the men at the barber shop to see if they will have an issue with their wives making more money.

RT: I guarantee it won't be a problem. Not these days. No. No. No. It's 2015 and women out here are getting bread. I've heard dudes talk about women owning tax offices, running small business, and advancing in their careers. Men do not care.

Plus just because he makes more money doesn't make him "the man" or "the head".

Somebody Shoulda Told Me

Although you prepare to have financial security in your life by graduating high school and attending college does not mean you will not come up against a financial storm in your life to include your marriage. When you are standing in the eye of the storm there are a particular set of skills you must have to ensure you don't get caught up in the cyclone. Those skills consist of communication, understanding, will power, negotiating, support, etc. In this time of turmoil, you have to remain focused on God and remember to put your trust in God and not man (woman). It's important to keep your focus on God and the faith you have in Him. Yes, it does take man to work but in the meantime you better sit at the hem of his garment…lol.

It is important that you not view your spouse as a failure, bomb, or a disappointment. If your financial woes are present due to an unemployed spouse, it is the working spouse's responsibility to be supportive and love them through the situation. This applies if they are working but not making the amount of money you think they should or that they are capable of making. We have an obligation to our spouse to help them reach their destiny, goals, and dreams. The unemployed spouse must be willing to accept the advice and support being offered. This is not the time to fight, verbally or physically, with each other. During a financial setback somebody shoulda told me if you are not in control of the situation you too can become estranged under the same roof.

Financial struggles or misunderstandings can destroy a marriage especially if the foundation of your relationship is already weak. Husband and wife must be on one accord with the vision for their family. In a relationship no one can feel "entitled" and surely cannot be selfish.

Somebody Shoulda Told Me that the issues of finances is a SERIOUS conversation that you MUST have prior to standing at the altar. You ask and answer theses questions……Who is going to be responsible for managing the home finances? What will we do if one of us loses our job? Promise never to.....

Somebody Shoulda Told Me that although you may have a fixed mindset based on what you discussed prior to marriage you have to be willing to adjust and respond to challenges as they present themselves. You can't be steadfast in a decision that is no longer working. As two lives try to mesh into one, changes in your mindset will happen. If you observe that your original plans and marriage are falling apart, you have to make a decision to look at a new way of operating. Strategy. Strategy. Strategy. This is the time when you have to come together and have each other's front, back, side-to-side.

There is scripture to support women's inner belief that our husband should be the provider, offer protection, and leadership for the home. The primary responsibility of the husband is to be a leader. Therefore, if the husband is the one not pulling his weight, the wife will seem irritable, frustrated, discombobulated, and maybe even angry. Men, you must understand her outward responses are a reflection of the pain she is suffering. You are able to calm those emotions with reassurance, diligence in making the situation better, loving on her, and being the best man you can be at the time. Colossians 3:19 says, *Husbands, love your wives and do not be harsh with them.*

Financial issues are not things you can ignore. Not talking about it is not going to help your marriage. We would like to advise you to be proactive rather than reactive. If you are reacting more than likely something has happened, tempers and attitudes are bad, and you will say things you really don't mean just because you are responding from hurt.

This is not the time to address your issue and concerns because neither person is really listening. If you want to be heard, you need to speak up in those moments when tension is low or not present.

RT: Men, it is extremely important for you to ask your woman what are her expectations and needs of you when it comes to finances. If you have not gotten married yet, ASK NOW. If you are married but have not faced a financial turbulence, ASK NOW. If you are in a marriage and been through the storm but you all have not had this discussion, ASK NOW. Men you must really understand your wife/girlfriend mindset when it deals with you and money.

CT: Women you must be aware of how your words and actions are affecting your man. If you are bombarding him with insults and innuendos you are ripping him of his pride, self-esteem and manhood. And that is something you cannot do. No matter how bad it gets, you are never to degrade your husband. You should not want to make him feel inferior to you. Proverbs 25:24 says, "Better to live on a corner of the roof than share a house with a quarrelsome wife." God placed you here to be his help mate, to offer counsel and advice. Once you show him that you have lost respect for him, the feelings become mutual and you will soon notice that he has also lost respect for you. Financial struggles cannot only destroy your marriage but it can destroy the relationship that you all have with one another.

Advice
1. Have a family plan
2. Know your spouse's expectations
3. Communicate (talk and listen)
4. Find another couple that is financially secure and pick their brains on how to overcome a financial strain on your marriage.
5. Be willing to adjust to make the situation better.

FYI: Financial issues are not only due to lack of money. That is just the route we have experienced and wanted to discuss. Other financial issues could be overspending, occurring debts, or one spouse lack of access to the money.

Chapter 8

EXPECTATIONS

The LORD God said, "It is not good for the man to be alone. I will make a helper suitable for him." Genesis 2:18

There was a survey conducted that stated 45% of the participants claimed unrealistic expectations as the reason for divorce. So let's explore how and why this is possible. Your expectations of your spouse and marriage in general will be based on what you saw and/or heard during your childhood years. Expectations can also form based on what you didn't see.

The outlook you have on your spouse is created based on the relationship you had with the parent of the same sex. The good qualities you observe are things you obviously want to experience in your marriage and see within your spouse. But understand the negative behavior you witness also influences your way of thinking. Although you may say you don't want a spouse that acts a certain way, unconsciously you may tend to attract someone that exhibit those very characteristics and traits. Familiarity and normality seems right, even when it's wrong. Especially if that's what you have been surrounded with for eighteen years of your life.

Think about the marriages you saw growing up. These examples are where you learned what is expected and acceptable. (But when you know better, you do better than perhaps they did.) What did you learn about relationships and expectations from watching those couples interact or not interact with one another? How many would you say were truly happy? How many were living together physically but divorced mentally? From the relationships that were the closest to you, what expectations did you bring from their marriage into your marriage? Do you expect a man to pay all the bills? Do you except your wife to run the house duties solo? Do you accept verbal or physical abuse?

We both came from two family households, parents married over twenty years at the time of our marriage conception. But their relationships were different in many ways, so we both brought two different mindsets into a union where we had to become ONE. This is one area of our relationship where we did have a few conversations during our ten month engagement. And we still had bumps in the road!

Our personal story....

I (Candace) based the role of the man off the presence of my father. My father was a provider. He was a handy man. He worked every day and I never experienced my parents struggle, financially. A man should always have a job to make sure his wife and kids have a roof over their head and food on the table. His wife should feel secure trusting her future with him. Yes, those where my thoughts and expectations. And not being willing to accept otherwise had a detrimental impact on my marriage. My father fixes any and everything inside and outside our home. And that's not only because he could but he has a frugal bone in his body!

    I was/am such a daddy's girl that I watched and learned from him all the time. I have changed my own oil and tires. I'm a lot like my daddy. I expected my husband to be a fixer. It is his job to take care of the maintenance of the house and cars. He was my example of how a man treats a woman. I cannot recall one argument between my parents, I've never heard my father curse at my mother or disrespect her in any manner. I'm not saying it didn't happen but I never saw it. The first time I knew my father cursed was when he asked me to read a letter he had written and it had a "little" curse word in it and I thought, "Oh, my goodness my daddy wrote a curse word". I was either a senior or in my first years of college when I read it. My father NEVER cursed at me, raised his voice at me (expect on the basketball court), belittled me, or talked crazy to me. He always made me feel like a precious jewel so why would I expect anything less from another man? Therefore, verbal or physical abuse in a relationships would never be tolerated. About five years into our marriage I decided to start dismissing myself from our arguments when curse words started to fly...I ain't gon' be able to do it!

    My (Remon) personal input is what I eluded to earlier--your expectations were molded based off what you saw growing up. But, you will learn quickly in a marriage is this: what worked for your mom and dad may not work for you. That will come with experience. It is due to you and your spouse having different personalities and coming from two different worlds. Growing up I didn't see my parents fight either, they told us they did early on but I don't remember it. There was never any physical altercations by any means. My mother kept a clean house. We could not go to bed with the kitchen dirty. My mother and father both cooked. They would walk in the house and immediately start prepping for dinner to be cooked. My mother always made sure my father had something for lunch. My parents worked TOGETHER as a unit! My mother didn't have to do anything pertaining to the outside of the house or automobiles. As far as inside the house, they worked together to build a home that magnified love and respect for one another. My parents truly worked as a team. If my father's work scheduled changed and he arrived home first, he would cook so she didn't have to. So entering my marriage I expected the same thing.

CAN YOU HAVE UNREALISTIC EXPECTATIONS OF YOUR SPOUSE?

RT: Yes you can have unrealistic expectations of your spouse. You have to know the person you are married to. You have be honest about what they are good at and what sucks. Why would you expect your wife to be responsible for paying the bills when she is a shop-a-holic and remembering deadlines is not on her priority list?! Re-evaluate your expectations. We need to stop trying to expect our spouses to do things we know is challenging for them. Yes, they probably could learn to do it or improve on it, but if you can do it better without much effort why is the demand there for them to do it?

Let's be clear. You should try to meet your spouse's expectations. If they have expressed a feeling or task that they need from you, it is your responsibility to attempt to please them. Men, we can have an unrealistic expectations when it comes to sex. We want it and need it every day. Truth-be-told to expect sex everyday with all that she has to do it can be a big requirement. Depending on the couple, creating an unrealistic list of expectations could be as long as the Great Wall of China, so I'm not going to go there. In your marriage, make sure you are honest with yourself and your spouse, communicate your capabilities with your spouse, have a good understanding, and put forth some effort. I believe if you do these things and your spouse observes you putting forth a genuine effort to meet their expectations will transcend a million miles away. If you want to really tick your spouse off, let them express to you something they sincerely need or want from you and you show no signs of even trying to do it.

CT: Sometimes women feel like their husbands have unrealistic expectations. And it goes a little something like this....she is expected to be the first up, fix breakfast for the kids, get the kids ready, work an eight hour shift, come home and cook and clean, make sure the kids are ready for bed, AND THEN take care of him. A woman has so many roles. She is expected to take kids to the doctor, attend birthday parties, attend practices, shop for the kids... THIS LIST can go on-and-on. And when you have a husband that believes all that is his wife job, my God, I feel sorry for her. Fellas, we are here to be your helpmate not a slave or maid. As my husband stated earlier, we are supposed to be working together.

Now if in your home you choose to have traditional roles and all I listed works for you and yours, I'm not speaking about you. I'm talking about the woman who wants her husband to relieve her from some of his expectations and help out more. Animosity brews within the spirit of a spouse drowning and seeking help when his/her spouse is unwilling to throw a life preserver. Everyone wants to feel valued in the relationship, and when you refuse to help it makes you feel unloved or like they don't love you enough to do "this".

Not only can you have unrealistic expectations of your spouse, but I believe you can have unrealistic expectations of your marriage. One unrealistic expectation is to believe that you should never experience some low moments in your marriage. When you bring two people from two different household together and try to mesh into one, there will be some valleys and growing pains to endure. The key is to learn from the experiences and grow TOGETHER.

Another unrealistic thought is that once you get married you are going to change someone. You might as well cast that thought/plan in the pits of Hell because it ain't going to happen. People don't change unless they want to. You can give all the ultimatums you want, if it isn't in their heart it will not happen. As a youngin', we think we can change people by treating them a certain way, giving threats, etc. When you been married for thirteen years you recognize you do not have power over anyone but yourself.

ARE THERE ANY UNREALISTIC EXPECTATIONS AS IT PERTAINS TO MARRIAGE?

RT: For a woman to think a man should pay every single bill in the house and she doesn't have to work is ludicrous and unrealistic in today's society. You need two incomes unless he is well into six-figures. A man should not be expected to pay every single bill in the household—especially if you have kids. It's too expensive out here to live off one salary.

CT: I think it's unrealistic for any one person to hold it down an extended period of time, husband or wife.

RT: I think it's unrealistic for men to think a woman is supposed to do everything when she comes home from work like she doesn't get tired. It's not wise to think a woman should cook, clean, and take care of the kids when she gets home while the husband kicks back and watches Sports Center. If you want a happy wife you better get up and help out.

C.T: PREACH! And let's also not be unrealistic by believing your spouse should have all the qualities of your parent of the same sex. This occurs when you have good parents and you want someone with those same qualities. And please don't ever say, "You are not like my mama" or "You are not like my daddy". That's another guaranteed way to tick your spouse smooth off. I do not see anything wrong with wanting your mate to possess the good qualities of your parent, but never make the mistake of comparing the two.

Somebody Shoulda Told Me

Somebody Shoulda Told Me that the expectations you have for your marriage or spouse will surely change from the day you got married. It will change because of trials, unexpected experiences, individual growth, and the directions in which you want your marriage to go. Somebody shoulda told me that it is okay to veer off the path of traditional expectations to a unique path that works for you and yours. When you grow together, you will begin to recognize and accept one other's strengths and weaknesses. It's okay for the woman to be the handy "woman" around the house and there is nothing wrong with the husband being the chef of the family. The key is to figure out what works for your marriage, be confident in that decision, and defend your union in the presence of those that speak against the culture of your home.

Somebody Shoulda Told Me that your expectations should be discussed in detail BEFORE you get married. This is a serious conversation that you must have prior to standing at the altar. You might want to have it while you're dating so you can decide if you even want to be engaged to this person. And when we say in detail, we mean *in detail*. What are your expectations when it comes to MONEY? What are your expectations when it comes to FAMILY? What are your expectations for the ROLES each person plays? What are you expectations when it comes to your DREAMS? What are your expectations when it comes to SEX? The older you get your expectations may change. You may add some but you very well may take away from the list. With age comes wisdom and a new mindset is formed.

Somebody Shoulda Told Me that you should have expectations for your spouse. You must have standards. You should not feel guilty for the things you would like and expect to see. BUT, you must be willing to compromise if necessary. Be willing to come to a happy medium about certain things.

Somebody Shoulda Told Me that your spouse may not be able to meet all your expectations on a daily basis throughout the years of your marriage and vice versa. And when your spouse informs you of an expectation you don't feel you are able or willing to do, you must communicate your hesitation or reserve about it. Do not allow your pride to prevent you from communicating with your spouse your feelings toward their expectations of you. It is best to get out in front of the situation instead of not doing it, not communicating that you didn't feel comfortable or capable of doing it, and allowing the hurt to fester in your hubby/wife. The lack of communication can slowly kill a marriage. And communicating with your best friend, the person you are the most intimate with, can be hard at times but you must do it.

Chapter 9
QUALITY TIME

"The greatest gift you can give someone is your time. Because when you give your time, you are giving a portion of your life that you will never get back." Unknown

Quality time during the dating phase is plentiful. The whole point of dating is to get to know someone, therefore, you make it a point to spend as much time together as possible. You have date nights, attend family events, and attend friends' functions with your mate. You absolutely enjoy being with the person. Since you don't have property together, not paying bills together, and are not legally bound to one another your arguments are few—as well they should be—so being in the presence of your lover is like being a kid in a candy store. Before marriage you don't necessary think about discussing quality time. You are so blinded by love that you don't realize that once you get married quality time can potentially be placed on the back burner. When you become married QT can become scarce. This could be due to careers, kids, or on the verge of falling out of love with one another.

Couples please remember that quality time is always needed, in fact, it's actually more important after you get married than it was before. As we were writing this chapter we had an ah-ha moment...it's the times when our marriages are in the most trouble that we pull away from each other, trying to distance ourselves as much as possible, but those are actually when we should become intentional about spending quality time together. And before we go any further we might just want to say what quality time is.

To us quality time is when you set aside time for just you and your spouse and find a sitter for those kids! It's an opportunity to put on some nice clothes and go somewhere you both enjoy that will bring enjoyment and life back into your relationship or continue what you have. Quality time requires you to box up your worries and concerns for a few hours while you soak in the love your spouse has to give. And QT does not require you leaving your home. Basically it allows you to escape the troubles of the world and refocus on who and what is really important.

Our personal story....

We sold our home this summer and had to move in with my parents as we looked for our next home. Once we moved in with my parents, there were eight people living under one roof. In our minds we figured we would be there for 30-45 days max. It shouldn't take us long to find a house (we thought). That time frame came and went very fast, and we were like uh-oh we better start finding time for each other. We decided to get a hotel room once a month, for either one night or two. It gave us an opportunity to talk with each other, hang out together without interruptions, and love on one another. This mini stay-cations gave us an opportunity to recharge our relationship and solidify our love.

HOW DOES A LACK OF QUALITY TIME AFFECT YOUR MARRIAGE?

RT: When you are married AND with kids, your daily to-do list can easily be filled with everything but your spouse. The lack of quality time can bring about a disconnection in your marriage. If you don't set aside time for your spouse it easy not to notice a change in their spirit. You miss the subtle clues of pain, hurt, issues, and concerns. You are unaware of how their personal life is going. You need quality time to stay grounded in your relationship. The Bible says nobody comes before your spouse, not even your kids. As parents, you naturally put your kid's needs before your own. But you can't forget about the person you fell in love with.

CT: When you don't take time out for one another, it can cause you to lose focus on your marriage. When you are engulfed with the hustle and bustle of life, it is very easy to forget about spending time with your spouse. You end up being more like roommates than lovers. Two ships passing in the sea. Y'all are taking care of the house and taking care of the kids, but not taking care of each other. A lack of attention for your spouse can cause you to miss the changes that are happening within them. When a couple does not spend quality time together the other's needs may go unnoticed. In any relationship that is valuable to you, you take out time to nurture that relationship. The people that you talk on the phone with on a regular basis, go visit, have lunch dates with are the one you are the closest to. When you don't make spending time with your spouse a priority and nurture your marriage, you can easily drift apart. Finding yourself on two different boats sailing in different directions. But you could also be sailing in the same direction but you definitely won't be doing it together. Do whatever you need to do to keep your relationship on fire!

Somebody Shoulda Told Me

Somebody Shoulda Told Me that you must continue to date your husband/wife. Whatever you did to get them you must continue to do throughout your marriage. Even when times are tough and you and your relationships feels like the life is being sucked out of it. As soon as you get married, make a pact with one another on how often you will have a date night. Find a ritual for your marriage: spend fifteen minutes each night recapping your day (uninterrupted), workout together, pray together every night, read together, take a walk around the block each morning/evening, once a month share the reasons you appreciate your baby. The key is you must stick to it regardless of the season you are experiencing in your marriage.

Somebody Shoulda Told Me about The Five Love Languages and that there is a test to measure your love languages. We took this test online during a time when we were in a horrible place in our marriage. And after we got the results of the test it made perfect sense as to what some of our issues were. His top to love languages were my bottom two love languages and vice versa. So neither one of us was giving the other person what he/she needed to feel loved. I recommend you take this test together annually or as often as you deem necessary.

Somebody Shoulda Told Me quality time is something you have to put effort into doing once you have kids and a career. Make spending one-on-one time with your spouse a priority. Because the lack of quality time can open Pandora's Box in so many different areas.

(Remon) A woman's need for compassion, intimacy (not necessarily sex), friendship, companionship is a necessity. As a man and husband, it is our responsibility to fulfill these needs. As a young man, no one tells you your wife will need you to sit down and just listen to her and truly talk to her. Quality time requires you to put away your phone, get up from the computer, turn off the TV (unless you are watching it together) and spend it without your kids present. NO DISTRACTIONS. During this time, you both should feel like nothing else in the world matters but the person sitting in front of you. The benefit of quality time is that it gives you an opportunity to stay in love or fall back in love. It also allows you to gauge your relationship when times are tough. Is this someone you are willing to continue to grow with or do you realize your marriage is toxic and unable to be saved? (Hopefully after reading this book, you are at the point of wanting to save it or keep it going.)

Chapter 10
GOD'S PLAN

In Genesis 2:15, God made it very clear from the beginning to Adam that he was appointing him to the garden and he was to work in it and take care of it. He then told him to he could enjoy it all except the tree of knowledge of good and evil. To put it bluntly God taught man to work and how to follow before he gave him someone to lead. God laid the responsibility for the home on Adam, not Eve. That's why, even though it was Eve who took from the forbidden fruit and gave it to Adam, God came looking for Adam. God commanded men to love our wives in Ephesians 5:25-27: *Husbands, love your wives, just as Christ loved the church and gave himself up for her to make her holy, cleansing her by the washing with water through the word, and to present her to himself as a radiant church, without stain or wrinkle or any other blemish, but holy blameless.* He did so because men were to take the lead and show unconditional love, the kind of love Christ demonstrated for his church.

God's order consists of God, man, and then woman. We cannot leave God at the altar and expect to have a happy marriage. God is the head of us all. He created man to head the family unit so man is the head of his wife. This simply means man is supposed to follow God so he can lead his wife and she can follow him. Thus it states in 1 Peter 3:7, *"Where men are commanded to give honor to our wife as the weaker vessel, so our prayers won't be hindered.*

If we're to follow God's order in marriage, men must follow God. Women were not created to lead the family but to follow and be led by her husband. No one but God comes before your spouse— not even your children or parents. In the Bible God did not command women to love their husbands. But God did command women to respect their husbands. This is why Peter tells wives not use their tongues to turn disobedient husbands around but rather to use reverence (1 Peter 3:11).

If each spouse follows the command God gave specifically for the male and female, a couple can become the unit God intended us to be! Our mate was created to fit together with us in marriage. He knew that man was in need of someone similar to himself. So Eve was created to make Adam complete to help him fulfill God's intentions for his life.

Couples will face one or more of the nine issues discussed in this book. But if we follow God's plan and commit to working together during the hard times…the number of divorces will decrease and she will be all you need and he will be all you want!

Postscript

We pray that every husband, wife, fiancé, fiancée, boyfriend, and girlfriend who read *Somebody Shoulda Told Me*, will develop a relationship that will be blessed beyond measures. We hope that we said something that will provoke change in your relationship so that you two will work together to live the best life possible, together.

Please continue to pray for us as we continue to pray for you.

Love,

The Tucks